HOW MACHINES WORK

MOTORCYCLES

CHRIS OXLADE

SAUNDERS
BOOK COMPANY

Published by Saunders Book Company
27 Stewart Road
Collingwood, ON Canada L9Y 4M7

Printed in the United States of America

Library of Congress Cataloging-in-Publication Data

Oxlade, Chris.
    Motorcycles / Chris Oxlade.
    p. cm.—(Smart Apple Media. How machines work)
    Includes index.
    Summary: "Describes in detail different types of motorcycles and how their engines, transmissions, and structures work"—Provided by publisher.
    ISBN 978-1-897563-44-1 (pbk)
    1. Motorcycles—Juvenile literature. I. Title.
TL440.15.O95 2009
629.227'5—dc22

2008002403

Created by Q2AMedia
Series Editor: Honor Head
Book Editor: Harriet McGregor
Senior Art Director: Ashita Murgai
Designers: Harleen Mehta, Ravijot Singh
Picture Researcher: Amit Tigga

All words in **bold** can be found in the Glossary on pages 30–31.

Web site information is correct at time of going to press. However, the publishers cannot accept liability for any information or links found on third-party Web sites.

Picture credits
t=top b=bottom c=center l=left r=right m=middle
Cover Images: Main image: BMW

American Honda Motor Co., Inc.: 4, 5t, 5b, BMW AG: 6, Nick Stubbs: 7t, Amy Walters/ Shutterstock: 7b, Triumph Motorcycles: 8tr, BMW AG: 8ml, Baloncici/ Shutterstock: 8br, American Honda Motor Co., Inc.: 9t, 9b, Michael G. Mill/ Shutterstock: 10 inset, BMW AG: 10b, American Honda Motor Co. Inc.: 11t, 13t, Baloncici/ Shutterstock: 13b, BMW AG:14, Martin Prihoda/ Istockphoto: 15t, Phill Clarke: 15b, American Honda Motor Co. Inc.: 16, 17t, 17b, 18, BMW AG: 19t, American Honda Motor Co., Inc.: 19b, Chua Kah Chun/ Shutterstock: 20t, Stephen McSweeny/ Shutterstock: 20b, American Honda Motor Co., Inc.: 21t, Ioannis Ioannou/ Shutterstock: 21b, Ducati Motor Holding S.p.A.: 22, American Honda Motor Co., Inc.: 23t, Confederate Motorcycles: 23b, Kawasaki Racing Team: 24, Frank Kletschkus/ Alamy: 25t, Pasphotography/ Shutterstock: 25b, Fred Goldstein/ Shutterstock: 26, Intelligent Energy: 27 inset, 27b, Dodge: 28, rMOTO: 29

Q2AMedia Art Bank: 11, 12

9 8 7 6 5 4 3 2

CONTENTS

MOTORCYCLES

Modern motorcycles are extremely high-tech machines. Their powerful engines give them amazing acceleration and terrifying top speeds.

MOTORCYCLE TYPES

All motorcycles have a **frame**, two wheels, and an engine. Street bikes are good for general use, such as getting around town. Cruisers are designed to make their riders look cool! Giant **touring bikes** are for long journeys and camping trips. Sports road bikes and racing superbikes are for thrills. Off-road bikes are for racing on dirt tracks and for doing jumps and tricks.

Tires
Keep contact with ground

Metal frame
Supports parts and keeps bike rigid

Engine
Powers bike

Brakes
Slow down bike

▲ The Honda Fireblade is a superbike. It has a powerful engine, but weighs just under 400 lb. (180 kg).

◀ Racing bikes are as powerful and as light as possible. A rider needs great skill to ride one quickly.

▼ Off-road bikes have special features, such as chunky tires and high suspension for traveling over rough ground.

DID YOU KNOW?
Some of the first motorcycles were powered by small steam engines.

Long front suspension

Skid plate to protect engine

High clearance under body

MOTORCYCLE ENGINES

In most motorcycles, the engine is at the bottom of the frame. Big motorcycles have engines with the same power as those in small cars.

ENGINE CYLINDERS

Motorcycle engines come in different shapes and sizes, but all of them have similar parts. Inside all engines are one or more can-shaped **cylinders**. **Pistons** fit snugly inside the cylinders, and slide up and down. The pistons are connected to the **crankshaft**.

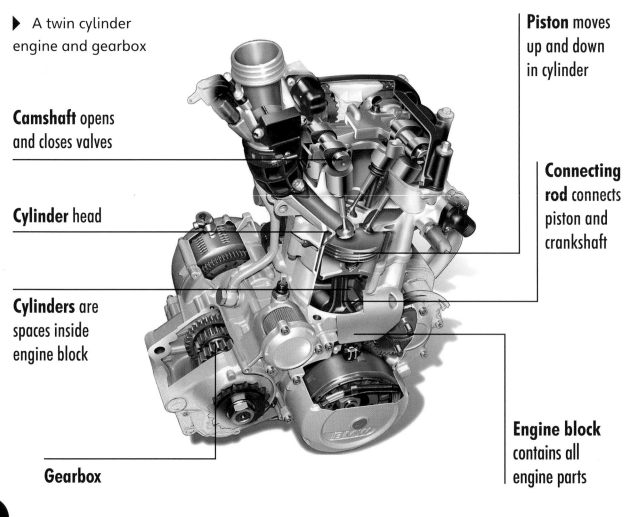

▶ A twin cylinder engine and gearbox

Piston moves up and down in cylinder

Camshaft opens and closes valves

Connecting rod connects piston and crankshaft

Cylinder head

Cylinders are spaces inside engine block

Engine block contains all engine parts

Gearbox

Fuel tank

VALVES

Valves open and let a mixture of fuel and air into the cylinders. Valves also let exhaust gases out of the cylinders. The valves are opened and closed by a **camshaft**. Exhaust gases go along the **exhaust** pipes and escape into the air.

▶ Fuel for the engine flows inside a pipe from the fuel tank to the engine.

DID YOU KNOW?
Motorcycle engines work at very high speeds. In a typical sports bike engine, the pistons move up and down more than 100 times a second.

Exhaust pipes

▶ The exhaust system takes exhaust gases away from the engine and into the air at the back of the bike.

ENGINE LAYOUTS

Motorcycle engines come in a variety of shapes and sizes. A **single-cylinder** engine has one cylinder. A **twin** engine has two cylinders. These can be arranged in three different ways:

1) Side by side (a parallel twin)

2) Opposite each other (an opposed twin or boxer)

3) At an angle to each other (a V-twin)

Many larger bikes have four cylinders arranged in a straight line (a straight four). The capacity is the total space inside the cylinders. A single cylinder can range from 50 **cc** to more than 1000 cc. One cc is one cubic centimeter.

▼ Some large BMW bikes have an opposed twin engine (also known as a boxer). The cylinders stick out on each side of the bike, next to the rider's feet.

▲ This is an 865 cc parallel twin engine.

▶ The V-twin is a classic engine layout found on many American motorcycles.

MEGA ENGINES

Big touring machines have plenty of luxury equipment and often carry two people and luggage. This adds up to a lot of weight. These motorcycles need big, powerful engines for good acceleration and smooth running on long journeys. The biggest touring bikes have six-cylinder, 1800 cc engines—bigger than the engines in family cars. The American Boss Hoss has a 5700 cc engine!

▼ The famous Honda Gold Wing touring bike, with its bodywork removed, is shown here. It is powered by an opposed six-cylinder engine.

HONDA GOLD WING

Specification

Engine:	opposed six-cylinder, 1832 cc
Power:	117 hp (87 kW)
Weight:	800 lb. (363 kg)
Length:	8.66 ft. (2.64 m)

Metal frame
Supports parts and keeps bike rigid

Large exhaust

DID YOU KNOW?
A large single-cylinder engine is known as a "thumper" because it makes a thump–thump noise as it works.

Three cylinders on each side of engine

HOW ENGINES WORK

The push that an engine gives to a motorcycle's wheels comes from small explosions in its cylinders. Most motorcycles have four-stroke engines.

THE FOUR-STROKE CYCLE

Each movement of a piston in or out of its cylinder is known as a stroke. In a four-stroke engine, a piston goes through a sequence of **four strokes** again and again. This sequence is called the four-stroke cycle.

▶ The camshafts, valves, piston, and cylinder of a four-stroke engine

Camshaft
Controls valves

Valve

Piston inside cylinder

Spark plug
Makes tiny spark that ignites mixture of fuel and air

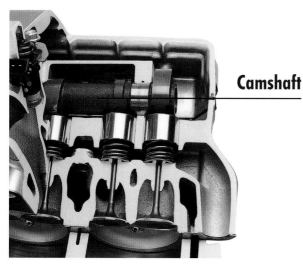

Camshaft

▲ A camshaft spins once per cycle. Egg-shaped pieces of metal along it force the inlet and outlet valves open.

WHAT HAPPENS

During the cycle, a camshaft opens and closes the valves at the top of the cylinder to let in fuel and let out exhaust gases. In an engine with two or more cylinders, the different strokes happen at different times in each cylinder, which makes the engine run smoothly.

THE FOUR-STROKE CYCLE

① INLET STROKE

The piston moves down, sucking a mixture of fuel and air into the cylinder.

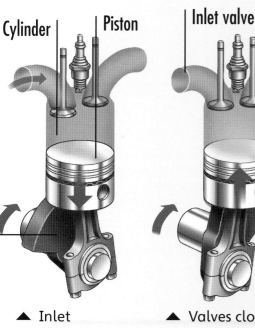

Cylinder   Piston

▲ Inlet valve open

② COMPRESSION STROKE

The piston moves up, squeezing the mixture into the top of the cylinder.

Inlet valve

▲ Valves closed

③ POWER STROKE

The spark plug ignites the mixture. The explosion pushes the piston down.

Spark plug Ignites fuel

▲ Valves closed

④ EXHAUST STROKE

The piston moves up, pushing the exhaust gases from the explosion out of the cylinder.

Outlet valve

▲ Outlet valve open

TWO-STROKE ENGINES

Some motorcycles have **two-stroke** engines instead of four-stroke engines. Two-stroke engines are simpler and lighter than four-stroke engines of the same size. They don't need a camshaft or valves. They produce more power, but give out more pollution than four-strokes. This is because the exhaust contains oil and unburned fuel.

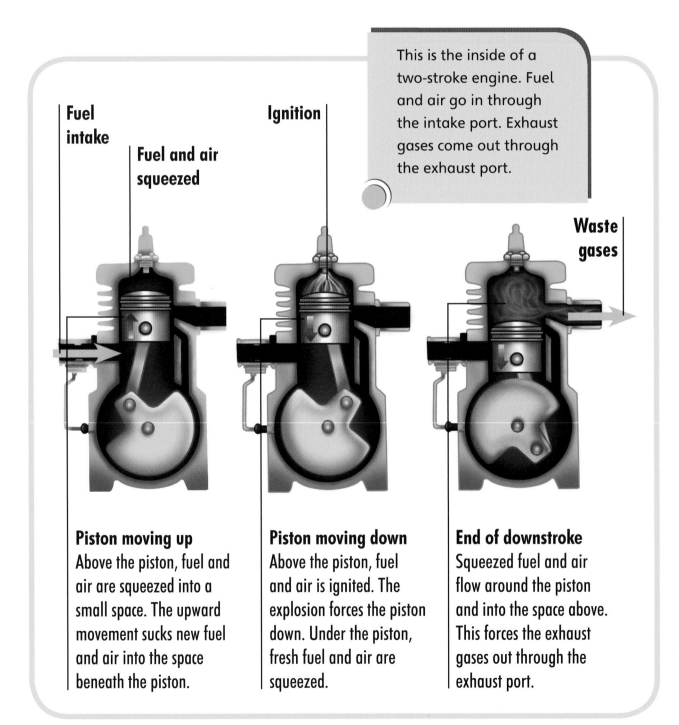

Fuel intake

Fuel and air squeezed

Ignition

Waste gases

This is the inside of a two-stroke engine. Fuel and air go in through the intake port. Exhaust gases come out through the exhaust port.

Piston moving up
Above the piston, fuel and air are squeezed into a small space. The upward movement sucks new fuel and air into the space beneath the piston.

Piston moving down
Above the piston, fuel and air is ignited. The explosion forces the piston down. Under the piston, fresh fuel and air are squeezed.

End of downstroke
Squeezed fuel and air flow around the piston and into the space above. This forces the exhaust gases out through the exhaust port.

◀ Two-stroke engines are often used on off-road bikes because they are light and powerful.

COOLING

When fuel explodes and burns in an engine's cylinders, it produces a lot of heat. Friction between the moving parts also produces heat. The engine must be cooled, otherwise the parts become extremely hot and the engine seizes up. Motorcycle engines are cooled either by water flowing through the engine block (water cooling) or by air flowing around the outside of the cylinders (air cooling).

These fins are on an air-cooled engine. When the bike is moving, air flows over them and cools the engine.

TRANSMISSION

A motorcycle's transmission is made up of the parts that connect the engine to the rear wheel. On most motorcycles these parts are the clutch, gearbox, and chain.

THE GEARBOX

A motorcycle's gears let the engine turn the rear wheel at different speeds. A rider uses low gears for slow speeds and high gears for fast speeds. The engine turns one set of **cogs** in the **gearbox**. These cogs turn another set of cogs, which drive the rear wheel.

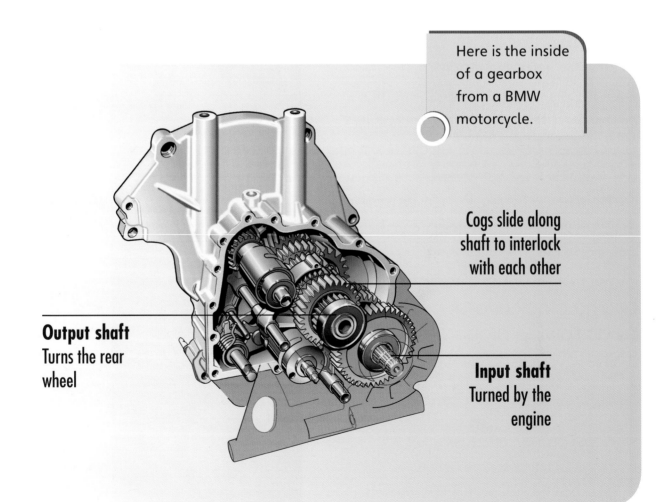

Here is the inside of a gearbox from a BMW motorcycle.

Cogs slide along shaft to interlock with each other

Output shaft
Turns the rear wheel

Input shaft
Turned by the engine

CHANGING GEAR

To change speed, the rider must change gears. Before the rider changes gears, the engine must be disconnected from the gearbox. The clutch disconnects the engine from the gearbox. The rider can then change gears. Large bikes have five or six gears.

▶ The rider changes gear by pressing down or lifting up the gear-change lever with the left foot.

DID YOU KNOW?
Motorcycles have no reverse gear, but some heavy touring bikes have an electric motor for reversing.

▼ A motorcycle clutch is made of two sets of plates. When the plates press against each other, the engine turns the rear wheel.

CHAIN DRIVES

Most motorcycles have a chain drive. This means the rear wheel is turned by a loop of chain from the gearbox. The chain goes around two wheels that have teeth around their rims. These are called sprocket wheels.

The front sprocket wheel is turned by the output shaft of the gearbox. The rear sprocket wheel is in the center of the rear wheel of the motorcycle. The front sprocket wheel pulls on the chain, and the chain pulls on the rear sprocket wheel.

Chain

Sprocket wheel
on back wheel

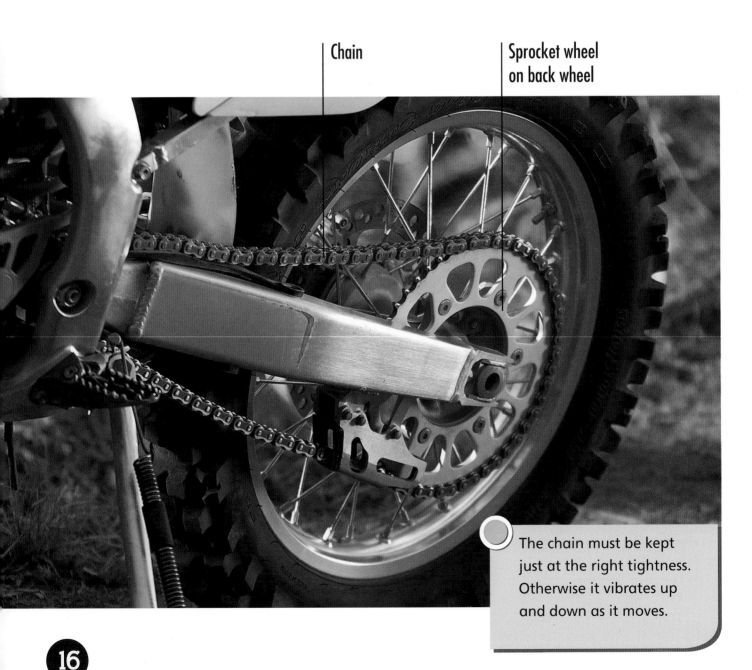

The chain must be kept just at the right tightness. Otherwise it vibrates up and down as it moves.

BELT OR SHAFT

A few motorcycles do not have chain drives. Instead, they have belt drives or shaft drives. A belt drive is similar to a chain drive, except that power is transferred from the gearbox to the wheels by a wide belt. In a shaft drive, the rear wheel is turned by a spinning shaft, or rod, from the gearbox. Shaft drives are quieter than chain drives.

The shaft drive of a BMW motorcycle. Bevel gears on the end of the shaft turn the wheel.

▼ An all-terrain vehicle (ATV) is like a motorcycle on four wheels. Some ATVs have all-wheel drive.

HONDA TRX420TM

Specification

Engine:	single-cylinder, 420 cc
Drive:	shaft drive to rear wheels
Weight:	522 lb. (237 kg)
Length:	6.74 ft. (2.05 m)

ALL ABOUT WHEELS

Tires must grip the road to let the bike accelerate, brake, and turn corners. The suspension keeps the tires on the road as the bike goes over bumps.

SUSPENSION

A motorcycle's **suspension** lets the wheels move up and down as they go over bumps. **Suspension units** have springs to let the wheels rise and fall. They also have devices called **shock absorbers** that stop the bike from repeatedly bouncing up and down on the springs after going over a bump.

Swing arm suspension on the back wheel

Shock absorber
Stops bike from bouncing up and down too much

Swing arm

TYPES OF SUSPENSION

Modern motorcycles usually have a telescopic **fork** suspension on the front wheel. They have a **swing arm** suspension on the rear wheel.

Off-road bikes have long suspension units that can absorb big bumps and heavy landings.

Fork

▲ The long-travel suspension of an off-road bike is designed to soak up the bumps on rough ground.

HONDA CRF450R

Specification

Engine:	single cylinder, 449 cc
Power:	51 hp (38 kW)
Drive:	chain
Weight:	227 lb. (103 kg)
Length:	7.18 ft. (2.19 m)

◀ Motorcycle tires have a rounded cross-section. This allows them to grip the road when a rider leans the bike on a bend. These racing bikes have smooth tires.

WHEELS

A motorcycle's wheels turn to let the bike move along the road. The rear wheel also pushes the motorcycle along.

A wheel is made of a hub and a rim. The hub lets the wheel turn easily. The rim supports the tire and keeps it in shape. Spokes are found between the hub and the rim.

▶ Road motorcycle tires have grooves that squeeze out water so the tire can grip wet roads. This is the wide wheel of a custom bike.

BRAKES

Brakes slow down a motorcycle. There are brakes on both the front and the rear wheels. They are both a type of brake called a disc brake. Attached to each wheel is a metal disc. Brake pads squeeze the discs, which slows the wheels. The brakes are operated by using the right foot pedal and the right-hand lever on the handlebar.

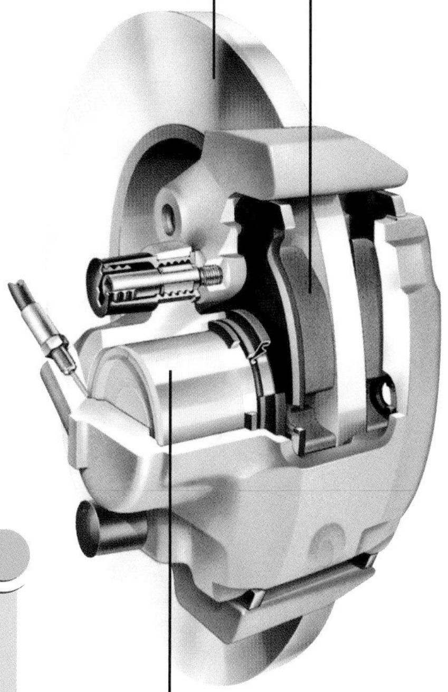

Brake disc attached to wheel

Brake pads

A cutaway image of a motorcycle's brake disc and brake pads

This cylinder presses the brake pads onto the disc.

▼ Shown here is the disc brake of a sports bike. The holes in the wheel let the disc cool after heavy braking.

Brake calliper
Contains brake pads

Brake disc
Attached to wheel

DID YOU KNOW?
Slick tires are smooth with no tread at all. They are used on race tracks, but only in dry weather.

STRUCTURE AND DESIGN

A motorcycle has a strong metal frame that holds all the other parts in position. A strong rigid frame is important for good handling at high speeds.

TUBULAR AND LATTICE FRAMES

There are several different types of motorcycle frames. Many motorcycles still use a traditional tubular frame, which is made of metal tubes welded together, similar to the frame of a bicycle. A lattice frame is made of two frames on either side of the motorcycle.

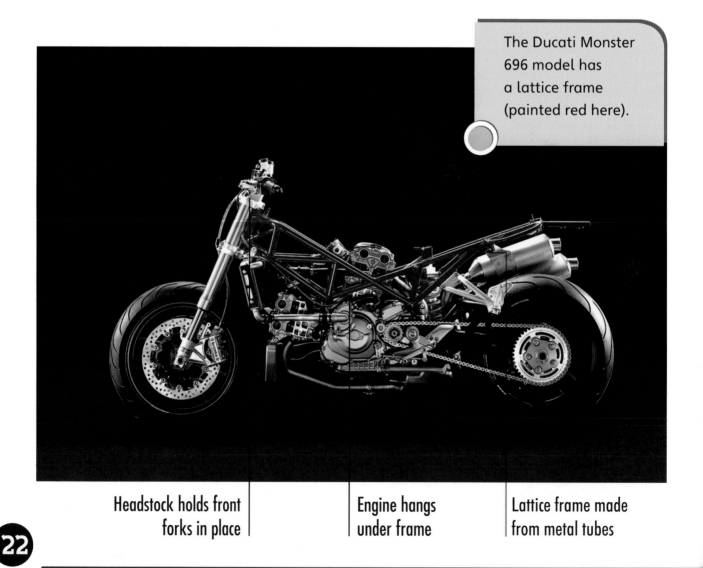

The Ducati Monster 696 model has a lattice frame (painted red here).

Headstock holds front forks in place

Engine hangs under frame

Lattice frame made from metal tubes

▼ The Honda CBR 600RR
has an aluminum perimeter
frame that supports its
powerful 599 cc engine.

Rear swing
arm

Perimeter frame
member

PERIMETER FRAMES

A perimeter frame is made of thick metal bars
that bend around the outside of the engine. The
frame has mounting points for the other parts,
such as the engine and suspension.

◀ On the Confederate
Hellcat, the engine block
is actually part of the
frame. It is known as a
structural member.

SHAPED FOR SPEED

Faster cycles, such as sport bikes and superbikes, are fitted with lightweight bodywork called fairings. This gives the motorcycle a smooth shape. It lets the bike cut through the air more easily than a bike without bodywork. It reduces a pull called **drag** that is made by air as the bike moves forward. The front fairing includes a low windshield for the driver to look through.

This race rider is ducking down behind the front fairing to reduce drag as much as possible.

Side fairings
With engine
air intakes

Front fairing
and windshield

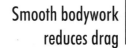

Smooth bodywork
reduces drag

▲ Motorcycles designed to break world speed records, such as this Ack Attack motorcycle, are fitted with an all-over fairing.

INSIDES OUT

Some motorcycles have no bodywork at all. These are not bikes designed for racing or touring, but for showing off on the streets! They are designed so you can see all the machinery that works the bike. They have large engines that make a loud roar. Custom bikes have many parts removed by their owners so that all the machinery is visible.

▶ The design of this bike is called a chopper.

Long forks

Stylized
bodywork

Low seat

NEW AND FUTURE CYCLES

Modern motorcycles have complex electronics that make them fast, efficient, and safe. Many features come from technology designed for racing bikes.

ELECTRIC MOTORCYCLES

Electric motorcycles are beginning to appear on the streets. These cycles are not as powerful or fast as cycles with gasoline engines. However, they are quiet and very efficient—perfect for riding around towns and cities. On existing electric motorcycles, the electricity comes from a battery.

An electric scooter is powered by an electric motor attached to the rear wheel.

FUEL CELL MOTORCYCLES

New electric motorcycles that are powered by fuel cells are also being produced. Fuel cells make electricity from fuels such as hydrogen and methanol. They are like batteries that can be recharged by adding more fuel. The only waste from a hydrogen fuel cell is water.

This is the fuel cell from an Emissions Neutral Vehicle (ENV) bike.

▼ This is the ENV motorcycle. It is powered by a hydrogen fuel cell. Trial versions are being tested around the world, but are not yet available to buy.

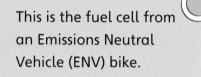

Drive belt from electric motor

CONCEPT BIKES

Motorcycle designers often design bikes to show what they think future motorcycles might look like. These cycles are called concept cycles. They feature incredible new ideas and technology. All of them look amazing. Some look weird. Designers show off their concept cycle ideas to the public at motorcycle shows. Most concept cycles never get produced for people to buy.

This incredible machine is the Dodge Tomahawk concept cycle. It features an 8.3-liter engine from a Dodge Viper sports car.

This is the Robrady rMOTO Electric Superbike concept. It is almost silent, but performs like a superbike!

◀ The electric motor drives the rear wheel. The batteries are recharged as the bike brakes and slows down.

THREE-WHEELED CONCEPTS

Although you probably think of motorcycles as two-wheeled machines, a few designs have three wheels. They are known as trikes. They are useful for carrying passengers, touring, and cruising. They normally have two wheels at the rear so they don't fall over when the rider stops. Designers have devised some concept three-wheelers that look nothing like any motorcycle you've seen before!

GLOSSARY

Camshaft Shaft in an engine that opens and closes the cylinder's valves as it spins

cc Short for cubic centimeter. Engine capacity is normally measured in cc or in cubic inches

Cog A tooth on the edge of a gear

Crankshaft Shaft that is turned by the pistons in an engine

Cylinder Can-shaped space inside an engine where fuel burns

Drag The pull that air exerts on a motorcycle as it moves forward. Drag slows down a motorcycle

Exhaust Parts of a motorcycle that carry exhaust gases away from the engine

Forks Two suspension units that support a motorcycle's front wheel

Four-stroke Engine that produces power on every other downstroke of a piston

Frame Part of a motorcycle that keeps the bike rigid and supports all its other parts. Also called a chassis

Gearbox Part of the transmission. It allows the engine to turn the wheels at different speeds

Piston Part of an engine that slides up and down in a cylinder

Shock absorber Part of a suspension unit that stops a wheel bouncing up and down after a bump

Single-cylinder Engine with just one cylinder and piston

Suspension Part of a motorcycle that lets the wheels move up and down as the motorcycle goes over bumps, keeping the tires in contact with the road

Suspension unit Part of a motorcycle suspension, made of a spring and a shock absorber

Swing arm Part of a motorcycle that connects the rear wheel to the frame. It lets the rear wheel move up and down

Touring bike Large motorcycle used for traveling long distances

Transmission Parts of a motorcycle that transfer movement from the engine to the wheels

Twin Engine with two cylinders and pistons

Two-stroke Engine that produces power on every downstroke of a piston

Valve Part of an engine that opens to let fuel into a cylinder (an inlet valve) or to let out exhaust gases (an exhaust valve)

INDEX

Web Sites

http://www.starmotorcycles.com/

http://powersports.honda.com/motorcycles/

http://www.kawasaki.com/Products/Motorcycles.aspx

http://www.suzukicycles.com/Products/Motorcycles/Default.aspx